CW01083513

Hard Light

Hard Light

MICHAEL CRUMMEY

Brick Books

CANADIAN CATALOGUING IN PUBLICATION DATA

Crummey, Michael, 1965–
Hard Light

Poems.
ISBN 0-919626-95-5

I. Title.

PS8555.R84H37 1998 C811'.54 C98-930473-6
PR9199.3.C78H37 1998

We acknowledge the support of the Canada Council for the Arts for
our publishing programme. The support of the Ontario Arts
Council is also gratefully acknowledged.

The cover is after a painting by David Blackwood,
'Splitting Table', oil tempera, 36x48, 1997.

Typeset in Galliard.
The stock is acid-free Zephyr Antique laid.
Printed and bound by The Porcupine's Quill Inc.

Brick Books
431 Boler Road, Box 20081
London, Ontario, N6K 4G6

brick.books@sympatico.ca

Contents

in memory of my grandparents,
Arthur Gasker Crummey and Minnie (Rose) Crummey

and for my grandmother,
Sarah (Reid) Sharpe

Rust

The boy watches his father's hands. The faint blue line of veins rivered across the backs, the knuckles like tiny furrowed hills on a plain. A moon rising at the tip of each finger.

Distance. Other worlds.

They have a history the boy knows nothing of, another life they have left behind. Twine knitted to mend the traps, the bodies of codfish opened with a blade, the red tangle of life pulled from their bellies. Motion and rhythms repeated to the point of thoughtlessness, map of a gone world etched into the unconscious life of his hands by daily necessities, the habits of generations.

On Saturday mornings the boy waits at the border of company property, rides figure 8s on his bicycle beside the railway tracks, watches the door beneath the deck head for his father coming off night shift.

Late September.

His father emerges from the mill in grey work clothes, a lunch tin cradled in the crook of one arm, his hands closeted in the pockets of a windbreaker. They head home together, past the concrete foundation of the Royal Stores that burned to the ground before the boy was born. Past the hospital, the hockey rink. The air smells of the near forest and sulphur from the ore mill and the early frost. What's left of summer is turning to rust in the leaves of birch and maple on the hills around the town, swathes of orange and coral like embers burning among the darkness of black spruce and fir.

The heat of their voices snagged in nets of white cloud. Their words flickering beneath the surface of what will be remembered, gone from the boy's head before they reach the front door of the house on Jackson Street. The mine will close, the town will collapse around them like a building hollowed by flame.

It will be years still before the boy thinks to ask his father about that other life, the world his hands carry with them like a barely discernable tattoo. His body hasn't been touched yet by the sad, particular beauty of things passing, of things about to be lost for good. Time's dark, indelible scar.

Water

I, Abraham LeDrew of Brigus in the District of Port de Grave, in consideration of the sum of Sixty Dollars ($60.00) in hand paid to me, have bargained sold and delivered unto Arthur Crummey of Western Bay, District of Bay de Verde: a Fishing Room with Dwelling House, Stage, and Store House at Breen's Island, Indian Tickle, Labrador, on land bounded as follows: North by Tobias LeDrew, South by Henry LeDrew, East by the Sea and West by the Sea.

To have and to hold the aforesaid premises unto the said Arthur Crummey, his heirs, executers, administrators and assigns forever.

In witness whereof I have herewith set my name and seal this 16th day of January, 1934 at Brigus, Newfoundland.

The boy is travelling to the Labrador as part of his father's crew for the first time. They have carted their gear down past Harbour Grace to Spaniard's Bay to be sure of a berth, loading nets, trunks, curing salt and barrels into the hold of the *Kyle*, settling clothes and twine over the mound of their belongings to make a place for sleeping. By the time the ship leaves Carbonear more than two hundred men and boys have descended into the hold for the voyage, a constant undertow of disembodied conversation in the dim light, fragments of a song rising from one corner or another.

Half a dozen Americans from Boston and New York sleep under cotton sheets in the first class berths. They drink twelve year old scotch in the saloon, brass polished around the bar, the dark stain of mahogany wood on the walls. They stand at the ship's railings in woolen coats to watch cathedrals of ice drift slowly south, a cloud of Eskimos coming down to meet the boat in Rigolet and Makkovic. They peer into the hold at the tangle of fishermen and gear, handkerchiefs pressed over their noses against the rising stench. They can barely understand a single word these people speak. A man from New England asks the boy to pose for a photograph, a school of Labrador islands in the background. His hands like snared birds at the ends of his sleeves, stiff, unnatural, he has never had his picture taken before. The photographer's tie is made of silk.

The boy comes above deck around mealtimes, stands near the dining room windows to watch white-coated waiters carry trays to the tables, spotless hands and sterling silver forks, mouthfuls of roast beef and mashed potatoes, ladles of gravy, cakes and pies for dessert. In three days he has eaten only hard tack and tea, his stomach aches like a tooth that should be pulled. His eyes water as he watches the food disappear, plates sent back half-full. The waiters carry in silver pots of coffee, after-dinner drinks; the guests push back their chairs, light up cigarettes, lift a casual finger for more sherry or whiskey.

The boy doesn't know enough to be angry with the way things are, wishes they could be otherwise in a vague unexpectant fashion;

turns toward the motion of the water, cutting his palms with his fingernails to feel the hunger less. He is three years younger than the scotch on the tables.

Making the Fish

Once you'd got the catch pitched up on the stage head, you got down to making the fish. Assembly line. Cutting table, blades of the knives pared almost to nothing by the sharpening stone. Woolen gloves soaked in fish guts, the water running red out of them when you make a fist. The cod passing through your hands like knots in an unbroken string as long as the sea is wide.

Cut Throat
Get your fingers into the gills of a cod and lift it to the table, 15, 20 pounds some of them and the ache in your arm after three hours like the chill in a church hall on a February morning. Two motions with the knife, across the throat below the gills and along the bare length of the belly, like a Catholic crossing himself before a meal. Push the fish along the table, the left hand of the man beside you reaching for it, he doesn't even turn his head in your direction.

Get your fingers in the gills of a cod and lift it to the table.

Header
The open body, the knife in your right hand. The head taken off clean, as if you were castrating a young bull. The liver scalloped from the chest and pushed into the oil barrel, left there to ferment like fruit going bad. The tangle of guts lifted clear, the cod flesh pulled from beneath, a body freed from a messy accident. Organs and offal dropped through a hole in the cutting table to the salt water beneath the stage.

The gulls screaming outside, fighting over blood.

Splitter
A good splitter could clear his way through 5 or 6 quintals an hour if the fish were a decent size, a full boat load done in three and out to the traps for more. Two cuts down each side of the sound bone, curved keel of the spine pulled clear and the cod splayed like a man about to be crucified. Dropped off the cutting table into the water of the puncheon tub, the next fish in your hands. Two cuts down each side, sound bone pulled clear, splayed cod dropped into the

puncheon tub. Two cuts, sound bone pulled clear, cod into the tub. Two cuts, pull, into the tub.

By nine o'clock it is too dark to see properly, eyes as tender as skin soaked too long in salt water. The wicks are lit in bowls of kerosene: oily flame, spiralling spine of black smoke.

Salter

Empty wooden wheelbarrow set beside the puncheon tub, the flat, triangular sheets of fish meat hefted from the elbow-deep water.

Dead weight of the loaded barrow a strain on the shoulders, the bones shifting down in their sockets, the tendons stretching to hold them as the feet shuffle into the store house. A hogshead of salt beside the bins, a handful strown across the white insides of each fish before they're stacked. Weight of the pile squeezing water from the flesh.

Turn with the emptied barrow. Squeak of the wheel, squish of feet soaked inside the rubber boots. Arm fishing into the puncheon tub, elbow numb with the cold.

The Bawn

Wait for a fine day in August. Sweep a stretch of beach clear, put stones down over any patch of grass that might spoil the fish.

The salt cod taken from the bins and washed by hand in puncheon tubs, front and back, like a child about to be presented to royalty, the white scum scrubbed off the dark layer of skin. Carried to the bawn on fish bars and laid out neatly in sunlight, 150 quintals at a time, the length of the shoreline like a well-shingled roof.

Two fine days would finish the job, a week and a half to cure the season's catch. The merchant's ship arriving in September, anchoring off in the Tickle; the cured cod loaded into the boat and ferried out.

What It Made

You could expect $2 a quintal for your trouble, a good season for a crew was 400 quintals. Anything more was an act of God. The Skipper took half a voyage, out of which he paid the girl her summer's wage, and squared up with the merchant for supplies taken on credit in the spring. The rest was split three ways. $130 for four months of work, it could cut the heart out of a man to think too much about what he was working for.

What the water does to your hands when you're fishing, well there's no telling it really. Blisters, open sores, cracks webbed around the knuckles, the salt water burning like iodine on a paper cut. Sometimes the skin roughs up, thickens into leather around the joints, you can barely close your hand to make a fist. The only thing for that is to soak them in a barrel of 'old soldiers': cured squid as salt as the brine and purple as a bruise, it's like losing your hands in a sunset. I don't know why that helps, but it does.

Water pups is another thing, welts on your hands and up your arm, the skin gone chalky white and a bubble of water underneath, you get those by the dozen. Some people say copper bracelets or brass around your wrists will drive them off, but I couldn't do a thing to help them until an old man told me to wrap my wrists with a strand of wool.

'And mind,' he says, '9 turns on each wrist. 3 is no good to you, and 5 is no good either. 9 turns of wool is the trick.'

I never had a problem with water pups after that. Used to strain my wrists hauling two or three hundred pounds of cod at a go, sometimes it got bad enough I couldn't turn a doorknob. That ended too.

Now you can wonder about it until your hair curls, but what's the point? If someone tells you to put your nets down where all day they've been brought up empty and you come away with a full trap, I say keep your mouth shut and be thankful.

The Law of the Ocean
Domino Run, Labrador 1943

The Americans had dozens of boats on the coast during the war years, surveying the islands, mapping every nook. They had poles erected on all the headlands with little silk rags at the top, forty, fifty feet high some of them. We had no idea what they were there for, but we stole every piece of silk we came across, carrying them down the pole in our teeth, they were perfect to boil up a bit of peas pudding, or to use as a handkerchief.

We were out jigging one afternoon, mid-August, the weather fine enough until the breeze turned and a wind as warm as furnace exhaust came up. Took in our lines and headed straight back into the Tickle, knowing what to expect behind it. Passed one of those survey ships on our way, holed up in a shallow cove and they hadn't even dropped anchor, just put out a grapple. We stopped in to warn them but the skipper more or less laughed at us, and the squall came on just like we said it would, the wind wicked enough to strip the flesh off a cow.

Next morning that little survey boat was sitting on dry land, blown twenty feet up off the water. When word got out, every boat in the Tickle headed straight for the cove and we made pretty short work of it. Took anything that wasn't bolted down, food, silverware, bedding, books and maps, compasses, liquor, clothes. Got my hands on one of those eight-day clocks they had aboard, but I was too greedy to take it all the way to Father's boat; hid it behind a bush and turned back to the ship for something else. And I'll be goddamned if someone didn't go and steal it on me.

The Americans were standing alongside but they didn't say a word. Law of the ocean, you see, salvage. We were like a pack of savages besides, seventy or eighty men and boys climbing in over the side, what could they say? Cleared the boat in fifteen minutes, as if we were trying to save family heirlooms from a burning building.

The Americans sent up a tug later that day to take the ship off the land and we all helped out where we could, throwing a few lines around the masthead, rocking her back and forth until she shimmied free and slipped into the water like a seal off an icepan.

We kept waiting for another chance like that to come along, but the Americans got smarter afterwards or maybe they just got luckier. It's a job to say the difference between those two at the best of times.

Grace

Indian Tickle, Labrador, 1945

There's no saying why things turn out one way and not another. It could have been me easy enough.

We were out after a meal of birds, took the boat around the head and a little ways into the Bay where they had their nests. Four of us, myself and Ken Powell, Bill Delaney, and Sandy who was just home from overseas. He'd brought a rifle back with him, a sharp double-barrelled thing with a German name, he could hit a turr at two hundred yards with that gun.

Sandy and Bill went ashore, and me and Ken pulled around in the boat to put the puffins to wing; they'd head straight for their nests and the other two would be waiting for them there. After half an hour or so we came into the shore to trade off, and Sandy passed me his gun as he stepped into the boat. Well, I can't say what changed my mind. I'd been after Sandy to let me use that rifle from the start of the season. Didn't like the way it sat in my hands and I stopped them just before they pushed off. 'Here my son,' I said, 'I'm not used to this thing. Give me back the single.' And Sandy passed it to me with this queer grin on his face, like he'd just won a bet with somebody.

We turned our backs and headed up the hill a ways, and then we heard it, a rifle shot but louder and not as clean, there was a grating sound like metal giving way. Sandy had seen a bird on his way off the shore, lifted the gun and fired. He threw it over the side and we never could find it to see what had happened exactly, but three of his fingers were gone, the bone of the first knuckle on his ring finger jutting from slivers of flesh as raw as a flayed cod.

The nearest hospital was in Cartwright, we took the boat and got started about six in the evening, going all night to Grady where we stopped in for a cup of tea. We pushed on right away though because Sandy's hand had come alive by then and he was throwing up with the pain, 'my Jesus Christ,' he kept saying, 'the fucking thing is on fire.' We had a bucket of salt water and that's where he kept it, dipping up a fresh lot every half hour or so, tossing the bloody stuff over the side.

It was ten days before he came back on one of the hospital boats, they'd sawed off the bit of knuckle from his ring finger then sewed him up, and he went right to work. I did what I could to pick up the slack for him, it could have been me afterall. You'd see that queer grin on his face when his mangled hand couldn't do what he wanted, as if he was thinking about those three lost fingers, pale as plucked birds, rotting at the bottom of the Bay.

When the Time Came

Well you didn't talk to children about that sort of thing. We found out when the time came, and I guess they figured that was soon enough.

This was in July and it was hot enough to split the rocks, I remember that. Father was away in Labrador. Mother was lying in her room all day, I can imagine she was overcome. And Dixon Crummey came to the house, she was not a regular visitor let's say. Late that afternoon Mother's water broke and I remember she said 'Dixon I think you're going to have to stay with me tonight.' Dixon made us our supper and got us into bed, and Mother lay in her room all evening.

What woke us the next morning was our sister, squalling. You can't imagine this, it was like she was conjured out of nothing, from the air. I walked down the hall to Mother's room and she was sitting back against a wall of pillows, holding a child. It was as sudden as an unexpected death and just as disconcerting. A sister is something you need some time to prepare for.

Everything was different after that, you could feel the order of the family shift, the way animals sense the weather changing. Mother kept to her bed for two weeks and Dixon stayed with us during the confinement, as they called it. When she got back on her feet she never strayed far from our sister; even when she was talking to you a part of her was somewhere else, attuned to something I was only peripherally a part of, listening for a cry.

And when Father got home from the Labrador that year his daughter was almost three months old. 'A girl,' he said, holding her in his hands, shaking his head and taking a good look. 'A girl.' The baby staring back as calm as you please, as if she could see the resemblance in this stranger's eyes and trusted him on that alone.

Fifties

After Father died I got a crew together and went down the Labrador myself; I was just sixteen then and the arse gone out of the fishery besides, it only took me two seasons to wind up a couple of hundred dollars in the hole.

I landed the job at the mine intending to work off the debt and go back to the fishing right away. One of the other stationers on Breen's Island wrote to me once I'd been gone five or six years, asking after the boat and the stage, said they were rotting away as it was. I told him to use what he wanted and never heard any more about it. I knew by then it was all over for me anyway.

My first Christmas home from the mine I'd gone up to see old man Sellars; he had me in for a glass of whiskey and a slice of cake and talked about forgiving some of what I owed him, but I wouldn't hear of it. Pulled out a slender stack of fifties and counted off two hundred dollars into his hand. New bills, the paper crisp as the first layer of ice over a pond in the fall. Then I had another glass of whiskey and then I went home out of it, half drunk and feeling like I'd lost something for good.

Earth

Bread

I was twenty years younger than my husband, his first wife dead in childbirth. I agreed to marry him because he was a good fisherman, because he had his own house and he was willing to take in my mother and father when the time came. It was a practical decision and he wasn't expecting more than that. Two people should never say the word love before they've eaten a sack of flour together, he told me.

The night we married I hiked my night dress around my thighs and shut my eyes so tight I saw stars. Afterwards I went outside and I was sick, throwing up over the fence. He came out the door behind me and put his hand to the small of my back. It happens your first time, he said. It'll get better.

I got pregnant right away and then he left for the Labrador. I dug the garden, watched my belly swell like a seed in water. Baked bread, bottled bakeapples for the winter store, cut the meadow grass for hay. After a month alone I even started to miss him a little.

The baby came early, a few weeks after my husband arrived home in September. We had the minister up to the house for the baptism the next day, Angus Maclean we named him, and we buried him in the graveyard in the Burnt Woods a week later. I remember he started crying at the table the morning of the funeral and I held his face against my belly until he stopped, his head in my hands about the size of the child before it was born. I don't know why sharing a grief will make you love someone.

I was pregnant again by November. I baked a loaf of bread and brought it to the table, still steaming from the oven. Set it on his plate whole and stood there looking at him. That's the last of that bag of flour, I told him. And he smiled at me and didn't say anything for a minute. I'll pick up another today, he said finally.

And that's how we left it for a while.

Root Cellar

A mound of sod like a single upturned breast beside the house, a three foot doorway staunched out with logs and two steps down into darkness. Dusty pungence, the warmth of must and dirt; the mossy odour of stored vegetables, that dull smell like an ache in your joints. The walls lined with barrels of potatoes, turnip, shelves of carrot and cabbage, a few beets, parsnip, radish, a sack of onions.

The men away in Labrador over the summer, planting and weeding done by the women and any children old enough to lift a trowel. My grandmother trenching half an acre of potatoes, carting wheelbarrows full of capelin to the garden, the slick silver bodies shovelled into the soil as fertilizer, the stink of rotting fish breeding a noisy pelt of bluebottles.

The late summer harvest stored in the root cellar and that was what kept people going through the end of the winter, potatoes still coming out of the cellar in March and April, brown skin thickened like a callous and sprouting wild white roots; the starchy flesh gone soft, gelatinous, like the eye of a dead animal. Potato and scruncheons, french fried potatoes, boiled spuds and pork fat, potato hash.

When Nan came home from the hospital the first time, she went straight to the pantry and peeled half a dozen new potatoes, put them on to boil and ate them plain, just a little butter and salt for taste. She hated hospital food, wanted something prepared by her own hands, something the earth had a claim to. The dry sweetness of them in her mouth. Feeding her body, feeding the tumour. She was seventy-one years old, her belly distended by cancer: six months they said, a year at the longest.

No one uses them anymore now, there's a refrigerator in every kitchen, every second corner has a grocery store. Abandoned root cellars still standing up and down the shoreline: hollow skull of sod in a meadow, a blank eye of darkness staring behind the doorway's empty socket.

Husbanding

I kept the animals until Aubrey got sick, there was no one to help with the haying after that. Everything else I could do myself, cleaning the dirt out of the stalls and milking in the morning, getting the cows in from the meadow before supper, it was something to get up for.

Spent a good many nights out in the barn too, waiting for the cows to calve in the spring. Sometimes you'd have to get your hands in there, the legs tangled behind the calf's head that was already hanging clear, a foot above dry straw, the tongue sticking out like a baby trying to get itself born from the mouth.

Only lost one cow in forty years of husbanding. Sat out there with her for hours that night and I knew things weren't right, the cow shifting on her legs in a queer way like a lady with a stone in her shoe, and shaking her head when she moaned. Around midnight she still hadn't started into birthing but she was bellowing loud enough to wake half of Riverhead, and trying to kick around her big belly. I sent Aubrey after Joe Slade to have a look at her, he came into the barn with his shirttail out and boots not tied; he didn't say much, just went away and brought back his gun and a knife. You can save the calf, he told me, or you can stand aside and lose them both.

I couldn't shoot her, but I used the knife after she fell, cutting away the belly to haul out the calf and rub her clean with straw. Aubrey brought a pail of milk he'd warmed on the stove and I fed the calf with an old baby bottle, the jerk of her head when she sucked almost enough to pull it from my hand. The blood, now that was something I'll never forget, we had to rake out the stall and burn the straw in the garden next morning.

Too much for one person though, the haying, three or four weeks in the fall to cut it and get it into the barn after it dried. Sold off the cows a couple of years before Aubrey died. I was sixty-one years old the first time I bought a carton of milk from a store.

Stones

A lot of it was learning to live with cruelty. To live cruelly.

We always had a couple of cats in the house, and the males you could do something with yourself. Father cut a hole in a barrel top, pushed the cat's head into it and had one of us hold its legs while he did the job with a set of metal shears. With females though, you had kittens to deal with once or twice a year. I drowned them in shallow water once, I didn't think it would make any difference, but I can still see that burlap sack moving like a pregnant belly only two feet out of reach; and I had to force myself to turn away. Those kittens were barely a week old but they took a long time dying.

The worst I ever saw was the horses. You'd get a strap around their waist with a ring underneath, and tie the fore and back legs to the ring with ropes. Then you'd back the animal up nice and slow so it would fall over in sections like a domino set, hind end first, then the belly, shoulders, head. Once it was on the ground you'd wash the bag with a bit of Jeye's Fluid, slit the sac open and snip the balls right off.

The cats bawled and screamed through the whole thing, but the horses never made a sound, they were too stunned I guess. Their legs made those ropes creak though, like a ship's rigging straining in a gale of wind. It would be a full day before they came back to themselves, standing out in the meadow like someone who can't recall their own name. Their wet eyes gone glassy with shock, as blind as two stones in a field.

Bay de Verde

At the tip of Conception Bay, a town built on uneven cliffs above the Atlantic, the scraggy red rock carpeted in spots with patchy moss. Moss can survive anywhere, and Newfoundlanders come a pretty close second I'd say. A few boats in the harbour now, but when I was young they were moored tight behind the breakwater like checkers on a board, dories and punts and skiffs, there were dozens of them.

A lot of Catholics down that way, but as Jim Crummey used to say, you can't hold that against them. Honest people in Bay de Verde. Salt of the earth. Went down with Jim one afternoon to sell a truckload of potatoes he bought near Carbonear for fifty dollars. The hill into town used to be as steep as hell's flames before they blasted through the rock, the brakes on Jim's old wreck squealing like the bell on an ice cream truck, half the town coming out of their houses to meet us. The first man wanted a barrel of potatoes, we loaded two burlap bags, passed them over the side, and while we waited for him to dig out his money started filling bags for someone else. When we looked up he was gone with the spuds. The next one gone as well, quick as that. Two dozen people around us shouting for potatoes, we just kept filling those sacks and passing them out, in ten minutes the truck was empty and we didn't have a copper to show for it.

Jim's face stunned, like an animal that's just been fixed. 'Jesus Christ,' he said, 'I'm ruined.'

I didn't know what to say to him. You could hear the gulls out over the harbour, the slosh of water on the rocks.

Then the first two or three people came out of their doors, the empty burlap bags folded over their shoulders. Then four or five more, then the rest, people lining up to pay with their fists closed around a few coins or a bill scrunched into a straw. When we drove back up that hill Jim had every cent he was owed and he never lost a bag besides.

Honest people, you had to give them that. And the shock of it all must have gone to Jim's head because he gave me a dollar for my help, and it wasn't even a full day's work I'd done by then.

The Burnt Woods

Picture him if you can, Uncle Bill Rose, great-grandfather, retired miner, handyman. Conjure a figure from the little you know. Black overcoat to his knees, a walking stick, the permanent hump on his back from an accident in Sydney Mines. The carpenter's saw your father keeps in the basement engraved with his initials: W.T.R.

Helped put up the United Church on the South Side as a young man, 15 cents an hour for his labour. Sailed to Cape Breton, spent his health in the mines picking coal. Half a dozen men from Western Bay killed in the accident that crippled his back, their bodies shipped home to be buried in the Burnt Woods.

Keeps a woodshop fifteen minutes from his daughter's home, he goes in every day but Sunday, opens the door on the scent of spruce gum, sawdust. An extended family of chisels in an orderly row on the back wall. He builds dressers, bureaus, knick-knacks. A pine border for his own grave hung in the rafters, planed smooth and painted years before he moved in with Minnie and her husband.

His wife has been dead longer than they were married. He will be buried beside her in 1951, aged ninety-three, a stranger to the woman by then, his time in the coal mines all but forgotten. The church on the South Side hills torn down one warped board at a time, the old lumber broken up for firewood and burnt. His lifetime of tools sold off but for the one handsaw your father took from the workshop wall to remember him by.

The middle initial on the handle still a mystery to you.

Jiggs' Dinner

Out of bed by seven to leave plenty of time to dress for church. The salt beef in soak overnight to take off the brine: put it on to boil in the largest pot in the pantry. Drain off half the salt water and replace it with fresh every hour. Clear a spot on the counter. Start the vegetables.

Potatoes
Potatoes are inevitable, like grace before a meal. You'll want a spud for everyone eating, two if they're smaller than your fist. The skin is mottled brown and spotted with eyes, the flesh is white and damp. The taste is neither here nor there, like its colour, it complements everything you serve. Cut the largest in half or three to avoid stony pits enduring after everything else is ready to eat.

Carrots
Carrots are the middle child, no one's particular favourite, but well enough liked by all. A good rule of thumb is to cook more than you think you need. Never worry about leftovers: a carrot holds its flavour like no other vegetable, it tries so hard to please.

Turnip and Parsnip
Predictable vegetables, sturdy and uncomplicated, tasting of the winter root cellar, the warmth of darkness smouldering beneath snow. Turnip is served mashed with a tablespoon of butter and a pinch of fresh pepper. Parsnip served like carrot, the beautifully tapered torso laid naked on the plate.

Greens
Leaf and stalk of the turnip, boiled until tender. The dark green of deep water shoals. As tart as spinach and better for you, the limp stalk wrapped around your fork like thread on a spool, a spill of green liquor on your lips with every mouthful.

Cabbage
Similar to lettuce, but heavier and more densely rounded: the

quieter and more secretive of two siblings. Too firm and fibrous to be eaten raw, boil the cabbage whole until the inner leaves have paled almost to white and part before a fork like the Red Sea before the staff of Moses.

Onions
Slip the pocket of tears from its papery shell. Do not bring the knife near the flesh. Drop two or three whole onions into the pot to cook the tang from the core. Eat them by the forkful, the translucent layers soft and sweet as orange sections, every bit of bitterness boiled away.

When the church bell peals, place all vegetables to boil with the salt meat. The peas pudding is wrapped separately in cheesecloth or a piece of rag and placed last in the pot, before leaving for church at a quarter to eleven.

By twelve-thirty everything is ready. Take up the vegetables in separate dishes and people will serve themselves as they please. Ladle a spoonful of the salty liquor from the pot over your food, or dip up a mugful to drink with your meal. Protect your Sunday clothes with a linen or cotton napkin. Bow your heads before you eat.

Be thankful.

Old Christmas Day

My father, yes.

Father died on Old Christmas Day, January 6th, 1946. We thought he was getting better, he'd managed a decent meal that Sunday for the first time in months, salt beef and cabbage, peas pudding, he ate the works. Mother used to make fruit puddings in the old Baking Soda cans, Hollis and myself carried one up to him for dessert. He took three or four mouthfuls from the can and then he slumped over in the bed, never made a sound. I ran across Riverhead to Uncle Wel's and burst in saying Father was dead, I don't know what I expected them to do.

Anyway we buried him. Had to take out the kitchen window to carry the coffin from the house and it was cold enough to skin you. Then we buried him.

I'm not saying this like I meant to.

He used to run a sawmill up the brook, it was something to do over the winters when there was no fishing. Mother made a fried egg sandwich and corked a bottle of tea for him every morning, we'd carry it up there together. It was warm inside from the heat of the machines running, and the scent of pine and spruce in the sawdust, I never smelled a place as clean as that mill. Father sat me up on the cutting table while he had his lunch and I usually ate more of the sandwich than he did. The first mill he had burnt down, the second one there weren't enough trees around to keep it running and he had to sell off the equipment or let it rust.

He worked hard is all I'm saying. The only summer that man didn't come to the Labrador he was having cataracts taken off his eyes. That was the year before he died, when he was sixty-two.

No, that's not it, nevermind, nevermind now.

Nevermind, I said.

Fire

This was before Confederation, so I don't know why we were being taught French at the school. We had a textbook called *32 Little Stories*. There was only enough to go around the class, so the teacher would borrow mine during the lesson and I moved back a seat to share with the person sitting behind me.

Kitch Williams would pronounce a word or sentence from the book and we were supposed to repeat it back to him, but I didn't bother opening my mouth half the time, it was all gibberish to me. Kitch decided he'd had enough of that one afternoon and got me up in front of the class alone. I guess I sounded a bit like a wounded animal trying to heave it out of me, it's a goddamn silly language anyway if you want my opinion, and the whole school had a good laugh about it.

Father had an old shotgun I used to take out hunting partridge on the weekends with Jeth Slade and Paddy Fitzgerald, a double-barrelled thing that hardly left enough meat on a bird to make a meal of it. The three of us went out over the barrens that Saturday and I took *32 Little Stories* along with me: opened it to the correct page, stood it up on an old tree stump, stepped back three paces and shot the fucking thing. Had to walk twelve feet past the tree stump to find it.

Next French lesson I moved back to sit at the desk behind me and Kitch Williams picked up my copy to start. The look on his face when he opened it: the book ripped by the lead shot, the paper melded together so you couldn't turn a page. The muscle in his cheek twitching, his eye glasses shifting on his nose. 'My son,' he said, putting the book on the desk in front of me, 'if you're not going to take care of this text, it would be just as well to put it in the stove.'

Mother always said it was a wonder I never got myself shot when I was a youngster. I picked the book up, walked to the pot-bellied stove at the back of the class and dropped it in. The crackle of *32 Little Stories* echoing around the room as I went back to my seat through the row of desks, the floor boards creaking under my feet. Quiet, my Jesus it was quiet, no one in that class had a word in their heads to speak, not of English and not of French besides.

Bonfire Night

Guy Fawkes tried to blow up the English Parliament Buildings with a basement full of explosives and got himself hanged for his trouble. Burned in effigy on the anniversary of his death in every Protestant outport in Newfoundland. No one remembers who he was or what he had against the government, but they love watching the clothes take, the straw poking through the shirt curling in the heat of the fire and bursting into flame.

The youngsters work for weeks before the event, gathering tree stumps and driftwood, old boxes, tires, and any other garbage that will burn, collecting it into piles on the headlands or in a meadow clearing. The spark of fires up and down the shore like lights warning of shoals or hidden rocks. Parents losing their kids in the darkness, in the red swirl of burning brush; teenagers running from one bonfire to the next, feeling something let loose inside themselves, a small dangerous explosion, the thin voices of their mothers shouting for them lost in the crack of dry wood and boughs in flames. They horse-jump an expanse of embers, their shoes blackened with soot, dare one another to go through larger and larger fires, through higher drifts of flankers: their young bodies suspended for a long moment above a pyre of spruce and driftwood, hung there like a straw effigy just before the flames take hold. Guy Fawkes a stranger to them, though they understand his story and want it for themselves.

Rebellion. Risk. Fire.

Flame

Breen's Island, Labrador, 1944

When we came home from the Labrador in the fall, we'd take down the stage head and cutting room to save it from the ice that raked the shoreline over the winter. Next summer then, the first thing you'd want to do would be to get the stage head back up and ready to go. There wasn't much in the way of trees in the tickle though and we'd have to take the boat into the bay to cut some timber and firewood. All day in the woods then with an axe, and the flies after your eyes the whole time; if you opened your mouth to speak they were thick enough to choke you. Before we went in we'd douse our hands with gasoline and sprinkle a little on our hats, it helped keep them off a bit. All the same, when you came out of the bay there was a solid flame of blood across your forehead, behind your ears and along the back of your neck, as if someone had traced your hairline with a razor.

The year Mike Tobin was up with us he soaked himself before we went in, he couldn't stand those fucking flies. I'd say he had enough juice in his hair to send the boat down to Battle Harbour, you could see the fumes rising from his head like heat over pavement. We split up into pairs then and walked in.

Joe Crowley was with him, he says they stopped for a smoke after an hour and Mike reached up to scratch the back of his head still holding the cigarette. We heard the yelling, and then we could see a small fire tearing through the trees toward the bay. He stripped off his shirt as he ran and he looked like a big wooden match, his head in flames above the white skin of his chest, a tassel of black smoke trailing behind him. It was funny as hell to look at but we managed to hold off until we got him out of the water and saw that he wasn't hurt bad. The hair was mostly gone and what was left smelled like piss on fire, but that was the worst of it.

Mike would've preferred if we never said a word about it afterwards, but it was too good to pass up. And Joe was the hardest on him. Everytime he wanted a laugh that summer he'd take out a cigarette, wave it in Mike's direction and shout, 'Hey Tobin. Got a light?'

The Tennessee Waltz

Ingredients:
  1 quart of dandelion flowers picked from the meadow garden
  4 gallons of water carried up from the brook
  2 and one half pounds of sugar from the winter store
  1 teaspoonful of cream of tartar, the rind and juice of 2 lemons

Boil the works in the beer pot for twenty minutes, turn it out into a pan and let it cool. When the liquid is new-milk warm, add four tablespoons of yeast and let it work for about a day, until you can see the tiny bubbles start to rise. Boil your bottles and siphon the beer from your pan, then cork tightly. Keep them in a cool place or the bottles may burst, the small explosions like rifle shots in the middle of the night, your shoes sticking to the floor for weeks, the house stinking of yeast and alcohol.

Fit to drink after two days in the bottle. A glassful will straighten a crooked spine. Three bottles enough to put a song in your heart and the heart of your neighbour come for a visit; four enough to light the flicker of dandelion flames in your sorry eyes. Five will set your head on fire, have your neighbour dancing around the kitchen with a broom, singing the only line he knows of *The Tennessee Waltz.* Send him home with one less sock than he came with. Wake you early with the tick of a cooling engine in your skull, your face the colour of ash. Your neighbour's wife wondering what became of that missing sock, and he will never find an explanation to satisfy her.

Makes about 3 dozen.

Bonfire Night (2)

They've swiped a cupful of gasoline – my father and Johnny Fitzgerald – doused a spruce branch and shoved it beneath the mound meant for burning. A match is struck and tossed: the suck of flame taking hold, the fire eating its way up through the overturned palm of driftwood and boughs, a cap of white smoke shifting over the crown of the bonfire.

Everyone takes a step back from the scorching heat, the crackle and spit of spruce gum burning. Night falls. Adults pass flasks of whiskey or moonshine, the flicker of silver making its way from hand to hand like the collection plate at church.

The boys have spent weeks hauling trees and branches across the barrens, scavenging rags and bits of scrap wood, but they aren't satisfied somehow with the innocence of the fire, its simple appetite. They stand restless in the dark light, their heads full of mischief: something they can't articulate is eating at them, burning its way from the inside out.

Match Avery steps up beside them like an answered prayer, breathing alcohol, nodding drunkenly toward the flames. 'Some fire,' he tells them. 'Nice bit of fire.' He blows snot into the crook of his palm, wipes the hand on the seat of his pants. 'All boughs though, she won't last long.' He nods again, emphatically. He's an adult, he's drunk, he knows everything there is to know about anything. 'Needs a bit of solid wood to keep her going,' he tells them.

The boys disappear into darkness, running a narrow dirt path worn through meadows. At Match's house they head straight for the root cellar like spilled gasoline rushing toward an open flame. They dump a summer's worth of vegetables onto damp ground, carry the empty wooden barrels back to the fire.

Match turns them in the red and yellow flicker, amazed by the boys' luck, by their resourcefulness. 'Now these,' he announces, 'are lovely barrels.' While my father and Johnny Fitzgerald look on Match stamps them flat himself, heaving the splintered sticks atop the blaze, throwing up a shower of sparks. 'Nice barrels,' he says again when he's done, and then wanders off toward another circle of light.

The boys stand together in the startling heat, multiplied now by dry lumber, the flames standing high as meadow grass before the haying. The bonfire goes on burning for hours beside them, dark flankers spitting at the stars.

What We Needed
Battle Harbour, Labrador, Early 1930's

Mother always said I would never find a man tall enough to marry me. People worried about those sorts of things in Connecticut. I left for Labrador at twenty-three, a green nurse standing head and shoulders over every girl I trained with and still single.

The first Newfoundland Ranger posted on the coast arrived a year later, fresh from three weeks of instruction in St. John's. A boat dropped him at the Battle Harbour wharf in October with enough rough lumber to put a roof over his head. The weather had already begun to turn by then, most of the fishing crews had scuttled back to the Island to wait out the winter. He stood there a long time, staring at that stack of wood, wondering how he was going to make something of it before the snow settled in.

There were eight men from Twillingate on the wharf with all their outfit: nets and chests, a few quintals of cured fish, waiting to take the last coastal boat of the season home. They were sitting on their gear, a few of them with pipes, halos of tobacco smoke around their heads. It was a Wednesday afternoon and the *Kyle* wasn't due into Battle Harbour until the weekend. He nodded in their direction.

It took them three days to put up the house, just a stone's throw from the hospital. He bought a new iron stove and a couple of chairs from Slade's, used a piece of lumber laid across wood horses for a table. He had no other furniture and there was nothing more to be had until the *Kyle* started its run again in the spring. He took a picture of the men beside the nearly finished shack, their hands stuffed down the front of coveralls, a blond spill of sawdust on their shoulders. Saw them off on the *Kyle* that Sunday, slipping the skipper a bottle of rum for the trip back to Notre Dame Bay.

A lot of things were done that way on the coast: because they had to be done, because there was no one else to do them. When the doctor was called away to other outports, the nurses delivered children, amputated limbs on fire with gangrene, sometimes only an ordinary carpenter's saw pulling through flesh and bone.

On the last decently warm morning of that year he saw nurses setting up beds to lay the TB patients out in the fresh air. Every fine day saw a row of them on the hospital veranda, below the inscription on the building that read *Such as you have done to the least of these my brethren, so have you done unto me.* He put on his uniform and boots, stepped along the path to the hospital and asked the first nurse he encountered about any extra cots he might be able to borrow or rent for the winter. When I looked up at him the heat of a blush flooded my face. He stood six feet six inches tall, a little higher in his boots.

My bridesmaids were the other nurses, and two men from Twillingate stood for the groom, dressed in their coveralls. He was relieved of his position for failing to remain single four years after joining the police force, built a small schooner and worked the coast for the Grenfell Mission, bringing patients from as far away as Red Bay and Rigolet for treatment or surgery.

We didn't have much back then, but we had what we needed. A house, a stove for a bit of fire, some furniture. A four poster bed brought in on the *Kyle* the summer we were wed.

...uth Side New school
...om was built in the
...ummer of 94 the first
...ayers was held on
...anuary 12 95.

The first Bell came
for the South Side

was in March 25th 1908
first time he rang in...
on March 27th 1908

Solomon Evans' Son

The graveyard in the Burnt Woods was being fenced in the year 1890. The first person buried there was Solomon Evans' son.

The new school on the South Side was built in the summer of 1894 beside the church. First prayers were held on January 12th, 1895.

The first church bell for the South Side arrived on March 25th, 1908, and it rang for the first time on March 27th, the peals as clear as the blue sky, the gulls put to wing by the sound of it, their brief racket like an echo rusting into silence.

The first time the bell tolled a death was for Mrs. Ellen Kennel. The school was closed for the afternoon, the children standing in the balcony of the church to watch her funeral, and some of them followed the coffin to the graveyard in the Burnt Woods. A hedge of people stood around the hole in the earth. The minister threw a handful of dirt on the wooden lid. 'Ashes to ashes,' he intoned, the October wind stealing the words from his mouth as he spoke.

The mourners filing out past the plain wooden cross marking the grave of Solomon Evans' son. Darkness of spruce trees, maples scorched by the coming of winter. And no one could recall the boy's name, or what it was he died of.

Infrared

A picture that was never taken, infrared photograph of the square wooden house in Western Bay, a record of heat and its loss. Most of the building sits in darkness, a shallow haze of escaping energy pink above the shingles, deeper and more insistent where the chimney rises into the night air.

Downstairs, the kitchen is a ball of flame, the draughty windows spilling fire. The wood stove at the centre, as dark as a heart, stoked full with junks of spruce and throwing heat like a small sun. The family sits as far back as kitchen walls allow, shirt sleeves rolled to the elbows, sweat on their brows, the temperature pushing 85 degrees.

In the next room, behind the closed kitchen door, a film of ice forms on water left sitting in a cup. Steam rises from the head of the woman who walks in from the kitchen to retrieve it and in the photograph her neat bun of hair is haloed by a shaggy orange glow.

Later, the outline of sleepers under blankets in the upstairs bedrooms mapped by a dull cocoon of warmth, a bright circle lying at their feet: beach rocks heated in the oven and carried to bed in knitted woolen covers. The outrageous autumn-red pulse fading as the house moves deeper into night, the incandescent warmth of it slowly guttering out into darkness.

Air

Her Mark

I, Ellen Rose of Western Bay in the Dominion of Newfoundland. Married woman, mother, stranger to my grandchildren. In consideration of natural love and affection, hereby give and make over unto my daughter Minnie Jane Crummey of Western Bay, a meadow garden situated at Riverhead, bounded to the north and east by Loveys Estate, to the south by John Lynch's land, to the west by the local road leading countrywards. Bounded above by the sky, by the blue song of angels and God's stars. Below by the bones of those who made me.

I leave nothing else. Every word I have spoken the wind has taken, as it will take me. As it will take my grandchildren's children, their heads full of fragments and my face not among those. The day will come when we are not remembered, I have wasted no part of my life in trying to make it otherwise.

In witness thereof I have set my hand and seal this thirteenth day of December, One thousand Nine hundred and Thirty Three.

Her
Ellen X Rose
Mark

Newfoundland,
Western Bay, To Wit:-

BE IT REMEMBERED that I,P.Wellington Crummey of Western Bay
aforesaid,Justice of the Peace, was personally present on the
thirteenth day of December 1933 and did see Ellen Rose,the
Grantor named in the within deed,duly execute the same by making
her mark thereto, the same having been read over and explained
to her by me, and she appearing to understand the same.

IN TESTIMONY WHEREOF I have hereunto set my hand the *5th*
day of *Sept* A.D.1934.

P.Wellington Crummey

Justice of the Peace.

I hereby Certify that the within deed was
deposited for registration this *12th* day of
October A.D., 1934 at *10³⁰*
o'clock *A* m., and was duly registered in
Volume *130* of the Registry of Deeds for
Newfoundland and its Dependencies, Folio *553-554*

Registrar of Deeds.

Procession

Mary Penny was twenty-one years old and almost nine months pregnant when she died of fright. A clear Saturday morning, wind off the ocean. Her husband away, fishing on the Labrador. She was carrying a bucket down to the brook for water, a hand on her belly, the child moving beneath her fingers like a salmon in a gill net.

From the bank above the brook she could see the United Church on the south side below Riverhead, the new school beside it. She kept her hand to her belly as she walked down the steep slope, balanced herself on stones over the surface. The bucket floated for a moment, then dipped and dragged with the weight of the water. She grunted as she pulled the full container clear of the brook. A stitch in her side moved slowly across her back, a thin flame licking at muscle.

At the top of the slope again she set the weight down in the grass, straightening with her hands on her hips, lungs clutching at the salt air. The sky was perfectly clear. She stared out across the mouth of the harbour, lifted a hand to shade her eyes. Her eyebrows pursed. There was a spot moving toward her, a peculiarly metallic smudge on the horizon that was becoming larger, more spherical. No, not a cloud, it was too uniform, too intent somehow.

Carried off course to the eastern coast of Newfoundland by a south-westerly wind over the Atlantic, the airboat was about to turn and begin a journey along the coast of the United States. In New York, a baseball game between the Yankees and the Brooklyn Dodgers would be interrupted as it passed overhead, the players and the crowd of fifteen thousand standing to stare at its nearly silent procession above the city.

It came closer to the spot where Mary stood alone, a cylindrical tent as large as the church, now larger, the sun lost behind it.

Her heart leapt in her chest, a panicked animal kicking at the stall door. The baby turned suddenly, dropped, like a log collapsing in a fireplace. She began running awkwardly, holding her stomach. She tried to call for her mother, her younger sister, but no sound came from her mouth; the shadow of the Zeppelin chasing her across the grass. Halfway along the path to her house she fell on her stomach, the pain pulling a cry from her throat. She lifted herself and began running again, the stitch across her back like a hook attached to a tree behind her.

Another two hundred yards.

By the time she reached the house she was already in labour. Bleeding through her clothes.

Old Wives' Tales

Except it wasn't a wife talking, or a woman for that matter. It was Charlie Rose at the house to see Father. I was only five or six years old and not even a part of the conversation, sitting under the kitchen table with the dog, listening to the men talk. Charlie said you had to get one before it learned to fly and split its tongue. Right down the middle, he said, and when the crow found the use of its wings it would be able to speak, Arthur, the same as you or I at this table.

You know how a child's mind works. The dog was just a pup then, three or four months old, a yellow Lab. A hot summer that year, we were sitting outside the day after Charlie's visit, her mouth open, panting, the thin tongue hanging there as pink and wet as the flesh of a watermelon. I loved that animal, I just wanted to hear her speak is all. Went in the house and brought out Mother's sewing shears, held one side of the tongue between my thumb and forefinger. The line down the centre like a factory-made perforation meant as a guide for the scissors.

What a mess that dog made when she drank, water slopping in all directions, her tongue split like a radio antennae, the separate leaves flailing as she lap-lap-lapped at the bowl. And not a word in her head for all that.

Two Voices

My uncle sits beside the wood stove in the kitchen, between two voices. On his left the varnished radio, on the daybed to his right his baby sister, squalling. *Look*, the radio begins, *up in the air, it's a bird, it's a plane ... it's Superman!* His sister screams into her red fists, a single unappeasable cry. My uncle leans toward the radio, the words distorted or lost beneath the baby's wail, like mice scurrying beneath a wood pile: ... *aster ... ana ... ding bull....* He cannot hush her or make her stop. *Able ... eap ... build ... gle bound*, the program is about to begin, his mother is elsewhere.

He stands over the child, stares down at her face, at the round open mouth like an entrance to a rabbit hole, a hidden creature crying from inside. He fingers a peppermint knob in his pocket and his hand suggests a plan, the candy about the size of the voice that will not stop: he drops it into the hole like a stone into a well, the soft plop echoing in the sudden, sickening silence.

Silence. He does not even hear the radio now as his sister's face begins to swell to the colour of a partridgeberry, a bright painful red, and panic enters him like a voice from the stars as the cheeks become blueish, then blue, and the eyes bulge in their sockets like snared animals. The entire episode of suffocation taking place in absolute silence, my uncle immobilized and staring stupidly at his sister, while behind him Superman goes on saving another world in silence.

And behind him his mother claps through the door, pushing him away and lifting the girl into the air by her heels, she is shouting something he cannot hear as she slaps the baby's back, and a wet peppermint candy falls to the floor, nothing, nothing, he hears nothing at all until the first cry, his sister's voice returning, the sound of her squall returning him to the world, to his mother yelling curses on his head, and the radio's bland conversation going on and on like a long sigh of relief in the background.

Your Soul, Your Soul, Your Soul

Uncle Lewis Crummey was the shortest man in Western Bay, five foot nothing and every inch of that was temper, we had a great bit of fun with him when we were youngsters.

After every snowfall we'd shovel a path from his house down to the brook so he could carry up his water, but we were careful not to make it wide enough for the buckets. Uncle Lew too short to hold the water above the snow, he'd get half way home when his arms would start dragging with the weight, the buckets banging the snowbanks on both sides of the path, slopping water, and he'd find himself standing in front of his door with empty containers. He'd have to turn around and make the trip over again, always with the same result.

We'd be watching from behind the woodpile to see him throw the buckets down and let fly with the cursing. God damn every long-legged man up in the Burnt Woods cemetery, he'd say. Aunt Sally would turn her eyes to the heavens if she was around to hear him, Lewis, your soul, your soul, your soul, she'd say. And the more she said it, the more Uncle Lew would swear. We'd let him make the trip to the brook five or six times before we came out from behind the shed or the woodpile and offered to get the water for him, as if we were just passing by and wanting to help out.

A damn sin what we did, the poor man dead and buried in the Burnt Woods for years now. Six feet of dirt for you up there, no matter what height you are alive and standing.

Kite

I was crooked as a rainbow when I was a boy, I'll admit it. Stabbed Hollis with a pocket knife down on the Labrador. Swung at him with a berry can and split his head open. He'd have beat the snot out of me on more than one occasion if I wasn't the faster runner.

He read something about Marconi's kites one summer and made one for himself out of brown paper and scrap wood; it had a tail ten feet long with bits of coloured rag tied every foot. He worked on it for a week in the old shed, and I chased him out into the meadow garden when he finished it. A perfect day for a kite, a brisk easterly and mostly clear. Helped him get it up and stood beside him as he let out yard after yard of string, the kite pulling taut like an anchored boat in a tide, the narrow wake of the tail snaking behind it. And I'm tugging at Hollis' sleeve, wanting to hold it myself; he's leaning back to keep it high in the wind and telling me no, no way, fuck off, it's my kite, no.

Crooked as a rainbow, like I said. I stomped off toward the house, wishing him dead. When I reached the edge of the garden the kite caught a downdraft, arcing to the ground like a hawk after a rabbit, as if my contrariness had sucked the very wind out of the sky behind me. It landed nose first ten feet in front of where I stood. Hollis was running in my direction, yelling something I couldn't hear over the sound of the wind and I wouldn't have listened anyway. So angry by then I wanted to do something unforgivable. Put both my feet through the kite where it lay and then I ran like hell.

Now he's gone I wish he'd caught up to me that day. Maybe he would have given me something to remember him by, the mark of his hand on my body somewhere. The thin line of a scar I could hold him with a while longer, before the sky carried him off for good.

Stan's Last Song

On New Year's Day the Orangemen gathered at the Lodge, their sashes draped across sweatered chests and overcoats, salt and pepper hats or bowlers leaving their ears bare to the frost. By eight o'clock in the morning they were ready to set out, marching down through Riverhead across the South Side hills, up every laneway, then over to the north side of Western Bay. The Catholics kept to their kitchens when they passed, thirty-five or forty men singing, their voices mapped by clouds of breath in the bitter air, cartoon bubbles holding the words of old Protestant hymns. If there was a lodge member who was too ill to join the parade, they stopped at his home to sing outside the fence, *I Need Thee Every Hour* or *A Closer Walk With Thee*, the sick man joining in from his bed.

After the parade, the Orangemen went back to the Lodge where the women had prepared a lunch. Soup and sandwich for a quarter. Then afternoon recitations, songs and skits, and Aunt Edna Milley would get halfway through her poem and forget the rest, every year it was the same thing, the familiar words fading like the faces of loved ones long dead. In the evening another meal, and then an after-dinner speaker, the preacher or Kitch Williams from the school, it was nine or ten o'clock before that was finished and cleared away.

That was when the Time really got started, a clap of movement in the hall, tables and chairs scraped back against the walls, people arriving from up and down the shore for the dance, Catholic and Protestant alike. A hundred people in the Lodge, the hardwood floor pitching and rolling under the stamp of feet. Stan Kennedy playing his accordion and calling out the square dances, *Swing your Partner, Now Step Back*. Stan was as blind as a stone, but he could play that accordion, his face lifted to the ceiling like a supplicant seeking forgiveness. Never had a lesson in his life, his body possessed by music, his hands pulling tunes from the air as people shouted out requests.

It was what everyone looked forward to, that dance. Stan played until four in the morning, he could barely croak out a word by the time we let him stop. The windows dripping steam from the heat of the dancers.

And the grey light of the moon showing the way home as people stepped out into the cold, their jackets folded across their arms, the sound of Stan's last song drifting to the stars.

Dominion

My grandfather paid $75 for the radio, it was only the second one on the shore in those days. The antenna was a Y-shaped wire strung between dogberry trees in the yard like a slender crucifix. The timid signals from St. John's or Halifax or Toronto gathered from the sky like prayers to the Almighty. The air festooned with words: News of the war overseas. Hymn sings on VOWR. Saturday night hockey games, the angelic voice of Foster Hewitt calling the play by play, *Hello Canada and hockey fans in the United States and Newfoundland.* That other Dominion. Half a dozen fishermen sitting around a draughty kitchen in Riverhead, Western Bay, in the District of Bay de Verde. Arms on their knees and heads bowed to follow the game being played in Toronto or Montreal, Boston, Detroit, or New York.

Bottles of spruce or molasses or dandelion beer, my grandfather knitting twine to mend the traps in the spring. A curse on the fucking Canadiens but they can play hockey those Frenchmen. Clouds of static when the winter storms blow up, every head leaning closer to the radio, a slender thread of air holding them to a world they will never see. The pictures they have in their heads of these cities like a blind man's conception of colour.

After the game is over, when the visitors have pushed out the door into the winter night, when the lights are doused and the family is swaddled in blankets, an oven-heated beach rock at the foot of their beds, the wind whistles through the trees in the yard, and the wind is full of words that only the trees can understand.

The dark mahogany radio sits expressionless in the kitchen, a little Buddha, contemplating silence.

Discovering Darkness

You happen on the book by accident, diary of a stranger long dead. Leaf through the pages, the photographs, buy it on a whim. At home you leave it on the coffee table and sit watching television, the face on the cover staring sternly at the ceiling. Your grandmother comes into the room and sits beside you; picks up the journal and looks at it for a moment. You have never seen her hold a book in her hands before. She says 'I knew him,' turning the book so you can see the man's face, the leather hat sitting crookedly on his head. When she was a girl in Twillingate, she worked at the grocery store where the old man bought his butter and flour: retired from the sea by then, his children grown and gone, living alone with his wife.

The book connected to you suddenly, the life recorded there a part of the world you claim as your own, the man's face a part of the darkness you come from. And when you begin reading it is partly your own story you find there.

For we are men of yesterday; we know nothing; our days upon
the earth are as shadows.

The Book of Job

All knowing darkens as it builds.

Tim Lilburn

'Magic lantern.' (April, 1889)

Bound for Great Britain and
beset by evening calm,
sails sheeted slack and lifeless;
the likeness of stars on the water,
hard yellow berries not ripe enough
to be gathered
Passengers and crew above decks
avoiding the breathless heat of their berths,
everyone wanting to be
anywhere but here

Brought out the magic lantern
and slides bought when I was last
in England, set it aboard a table
on the foredeck –
every head turning to
the breadth of the topmast
when the kerosene flame was lit
behind the lens,
the Tower of London standing
on the yellow canvas as if
we had dreamed it there
together

Flashed up the Crystal Palace,
Piccadilly, the National Gallery,
then London Bridge,
the length of it shaken by
a rare gust of wind;
and the nearly-full moon rose
above the topyard,
the *Doune Castle* lying stilled
in its light like a photograph
projected on the water

Learning the Price of Fish 1876-1887

'And now to make a start as a boy of very little understanding.' (1876)

After a single season jigging cod
I gave up on the ocean,
boarded a steamship bound
for Little Bay Mines where
I secured a position
picking for copper;
kept at it through the winter,
a long shadow working
effortlessly beside me
while my back was shaken crooked
by the jabber of pickhead on rock,
my hands too numb
at the end of a shift
to properly hold a spoon

In June I jacked up and went
back to fishing, shipping out
with a crew headed to the French Shore,
happy just to be on the water
after seven months discovering darkness
in the mine

Salt air like a handful of brine
held to the face of an unconscious man
coming slowly to his senses

'A hard toil and worry for nothing.' (1879)

Left Twillingate on April 15th after seals,
steering off NE through open water, arriving
in Quirpon a day past the Grey Islands April 21st.
Sailed from there to Green's Pond, then to Gramper's Cove,
dickering through slack ice until White Bay
where we came on a gale of wind and got raftered
between pans, the boat brought up solid
like an axe in a knot of birch.

Lay there a week getting short of provisions
and patience till the Captain decided some
would have to leave the vessel or starve,
sending six overboard with 2 boats and what food
could be spared. We marched south toward
Twillingate, hauling boats and supplies till
we came on a run of open water in Lobster Harbour,
rowing on to Handy Island before giving up for darkness.
Set out for a long day's launching and pulling
to Flourdelu at first light, the ice slobby and
treacherous, taking us through to the waist on times.
Next day on to Lacie, chewing handfuls of old snow
when the fresh water ran dry.

Our fourth day out we passed Cape St. John and
Cull Island where the schooner *Queen* ran ashore,
all hands but one coming across on a line
before the wind took her over. The papers reported
how they perished there, and published Dr Dowsley's
letter to his wife dated December 18th, 1867 –
my dear Margaret, I have been out to see if there is
any chance of rescue but no such thing   I would give
the world for one drink of water but I shall never
get it now   We are all wet and frozen may God pity
and have mercy …

I was sixteen years old, my first
time to the ice and I stared at the island as
we slogged past it, a bald crown of rock and
no sign of life to be made out there but shadows.

It was three days more past the Cape, trimming
the shore all the way through Green Bay nearly
blocked with ice; we didn't get clear of it
until Lading Tickle when a s w wind took it off
the land, we hung up our rugs for sails on the oars
and straightened them out for home.
Arrived in Twillingate on June 17th, our boots
sliced through with the rough walking
and blood still in our mouths from the snow.
And on the 18th our schooner sailed into the harbour
behind us, all hands rested and well fed, we had
a hard toil and worry for nothing.

'A trip to the Labrador among the Esquimaux' (1882)

Left home on July 3rd with Captain Abraham Herl
being my first start for the Labrador,
a pleasant breeze behind us and on the 7th
we stopped over in Indian Tickle, laying up
a night in the lee of Breen's Island;
then down as far as Hopedale among the Esquimaux
where I took a good view of their materials
passed on from the days when our Lord
Jesus Christ was preaching in the holy lands.
The people seemed strange to me as it was
my first time among them and I could not
understand their language which some claim
is descended directly from Cain
but they showed us many curious things
and I was delighted with them.
We stayed over a weekend and attended
a service at the Moravian church
where the German preacher offered prayers
in that queer hum rutted with clicks
and burps, and several among us thought
to be offended on God's behalf.
But he prayed for a good trip of fishing
for the visitors in a more familiar tongue,
our traps came up full off the Farmyard Islands,
and Captain Herl suggested God is not
so particular as some would have us believe.

'The price of fish.' (September, 1887)

I have had a fair trial on the fishing line now,
being 3 summers out from home, 2 summers on
the French Shore, 4 down on the Labrador,
and three trips this year to the Banks of Newfoundland,
and this is what I have learned to be the price of fish

Shem Yates and Harry Brown lost with the *Abyssinia*,
making through slack ice 60 miles N E of the Grey Islands
when the wind turned and she struck hard on a block,
the vessel split like a stick of frozen kindling –
May, 1886

Tom Viven out of Crow Head, his boat running
loaded down through heavy seas that opened her up forward,
going down just off Kettle Cove and a good trip of fish lost besides –
August, 1884

My last trip to the French Shore, Luke Brumley and Fred Strong
sent out to take in a trap set loose in a gale,
the rough weather filling their skiff with water
when they hauled up the span line, the two men
pitched under only a good shout from the *Traveller*
but neither one could swim a stroke –
June, 1882

Show me a map and I'll name you a dead man for
every cove between home and Battle Harbour

I am twenty four years old,
there is no guarantee I will ever see twenty five

Expecting To Be Changed 1887-1894

'On the broad Atlantic for the first time
to cross the pond.' (November, 1887)

When I signed on the *Konigsburg*
bound for Italy with
a load of dry cod
I had expectations,
but I could not rightly say
what they were

We hove up the anchor,
sheeted our topsails
and my family waved me out
of the harbour
as if they knew they had
seen me for the last time

I expected to be changed
and I thought a change
would not do me
any harm

'Names of the Ropes' (1887)

Now as the sails are set a sailor must know
all the ropes or running gear before he can
reef, clew or furl, and the names of the ropes
are as follows. Jib halliards. Troat halliards.
Peak, Royal and Topgallant halliards.
Royal braces, Topgallant braces, Topsail braces.
Fore and Main braces. Preventer main braces.
After main braces. Sheets and lifts for the
Topgallant, Topsail and Main. Clewgarnets.
Foretack, Topsail buntlines, Reef burtons.
Leech lines. Slab lines. Spanker's brail and
outhall. Boom topping outhall. Flying jib
downhall, jib downhall, fore topmast stays.
Which is not to mention the standing rigging
on which the sailors move among the ropes
in all weather and sometimes appear
to be spiders mending a web, while at others
they appear to be caught and helpless as flies
in a web of someone else's design.

'Crossing the equator.
Arrived in Rio Grande.' (1888)

Set sail from Spain April 24th,
arrived in Rio Grande after sixty nights at sea.
Discharged our cargo and proceeded up
the Port de Lego River for a load of horn,
hides and tallow, arriving July 10th.

In Pelotas fresh meat went for 3 cents a pound,
apples could be had for a good song
or a chew of hard tobacco and
we drew water over the side for all purposes.
Once our cargo was secured, the Port de Lego
carried us back to Rio Grande, groves of
green trees on the shore bowed so low
you could pick fruit from the branches
as we sailed beneath them; ripe oranges
went ungathered, dropping straight into the water
and floating downstream beside the ship.

When I was a boy I went aboard every boat
that sailed into Twillingate just to hear
the sailors talk; there was a man from Devonshire
claiming sight of countries where fruit is
as plentiful as cod on a Grand Bank shoal,
it seemed too fanciful a notion to put much faith in.
We stood on deck with buckets and nets
and we dipped them from the river by the hundred,
eating till we were sick of sweetness, stowing
the rest below for the voyage back to London.

'Arrived in Hong Kong, November 9.
The histories of China.' (1888)

Sailed into the harbour early morning
and made our ship fast to the old stone quay,
the Chinese coming down in hundreds to greet us –
a queer lot to look at I guess,
the men wearing braided pigtails
and the women stepping as if
they were walking on glass,
their stunted feet bound tight as a reefed sail

Went ashore after tea and received some peculiar looks
though I was turned out as well as a sailor can manage;
stopped into a bar where I checked myself
in the glass and found no fault to speak of,
perhaps it was my ears
they were staring at

Dusk when I found my way back to the waterfront
and three parts drunk by then,
14000 miles from Newfoundland
to the east and west
and can get no further from my home if I wanted –
2000 years before the birth of Christ
the Emperor Yu divided this empire
into 9 provinces and etched
their borders on 9 copper vessels …

The stars came out over the Pacific then
and they came out over me,
only 26 years old and all the histories
of China at my back

'The Fearnot of Liverpool' (1889)

On October 16th we passed a large bark
dismasted and abandoned on open water,
the main and mizzen down and
no sign of life, we lay alongside
several hours but could not launch
our boats to get aboard her
as there was a heavy sea running
and she was as good as fifty years away.
Finally we turned to and left her
adrift, with only our own stories
of what might have happened to ship
and crew troubling our sleep.

Continued without incident until
the 26th when I was on my way to rouse
the 3rd officer for morning watch
and there was a shout of man overboard.
We cast out the life buoys and
launched the lifeboat, pulling around
in the darkness until 8 o'clock
before giving him up for lost.
Put the ship on course and we were
now running one man short.
He'd done the work himself and jumped
though no one could say his reason
or what was in his head to send him
over the side in weather
calm as a dream of home.

'Arrived in Odessa, Russia. Bonaparte at Moscow.' (1889)

Winter defeated Napoleon.
Moscow razed by Russia's defenders
to deprive the advancing army
of food and shelter,
not enough wood left among
the ash of the city
to make a proper fire.

November fell like a building
hollowed by flame.

Hands and feet of the retreating soldiers
scorched by frostbite,
exposed skin of their faces
dead to the touch.
300 thousand men fell to
the cold and to hunger
on the long march out of Russia,
their frozen bodies on
the roadside like a knotted string
being unravelled all the way
back to France.

And Moscow standing again now,
spired and magnificent,
as if Napoleon had never lived.

'In a great row and got locked up.' (1890)

You may have all the pleasure here that
you need and you may get it as rough
as you please if you are not careful.
Lying near Fulton Ferry in Brooklyn
I went ashore with the other quartermasters,
a Cockney and a Belgian,
falling in with a crowd of bunker boys
at a barroom and drinking in the usual way
when a big row rose up that washed over
the entire crowd assembled,
bottles, trays, and glasses flying
as if the room was being rocked by a gale.
My two shipmates got the worst of the play
that was started on me, the Belgian's nose
was broken and blood all down his front
when we met up again near the ship,
and they blamed me for raising the ruckus
when I had all I could do to get clear
with a whole skin. The Belgian brandished
a knife and the Cockney did nothing
to discourage him when he swore he would
take my life right there in the street,
so I pulled out my revolver and fired.
Four policemen arrived thereafter and
they put me aboard the Black Mary to
take me to the lockup, I said 'Boys
I never enjoy a decent ride except
when I am driving with you',
they said I wouldn't think so by
the time I got through with this affair.

Next morning I was taken before the Judge,
the two Quartermasters and others were there
to give their evidence which was not
in my favour. The Judge asked if I was
guilty of the charge and I told him yes,
the Belgian had come at me with his knife
and I burned the skin of his forehead with a bullet,
upon which evidence the case was dismissed,
self-defence being the first point of law in America.
The Belgian and me took the day off
to go across the bridge to New York
where we had a jolly time of it since
sailors hold no malice, and then we sailed
back to England as friendly as ever
with a pleasant smile.

'Observatory on Mount Pleasant' (1890)

Paid off a ship in St John, New Brunswick
and no work to be had until I got word
of a building going up in Mount Pleasant.
The foundation already down
when I arrived and the foreman
took me on as soon as I mentioned
being several years on the tall ships.
It was twenty stories high when we finished,
and I was sent up the pole to hook the block
and hoist the framing for each floor.
Each time up I could see more of
Lily Lake at the foot of the mountain,
the crooked arms of the apple trees
laid out in orchard rows,
and there was always a handful of nuns
saying the Rosary outside the convent below.
I waved in their direction from every story
but they went on praying as if they hadn't seen me,
perhaps it was my safety
they were bringing to God's attention.
Stayed on until the place opened in October
and the night before I shipped out
they sat me in the chair beneath
a telescope the size of a humpback –
for the first time I saw constellations
the way a saint perceives the divine,
almost clear of darkness.
When I carted my tools down the hill
those stars came with me, a branch of
ripe fruit almost close enough to touch.

'A hard looking sight but not lost.' (1890)

Now I have been on board some hard ships
but this one takes the lead of them all.
They say there was six men killed on her last voyage,
the Captain changed her name and still
could not entice a soul aboard before
my chum and me took a chance and signed on.
We sailed into Bath Bay and took on
a load of ice, leaving again October 22nd.
The following day a wind came up with rain and thunder
so we clewed up the foremain and mizzen topsails
and had two reefs in the mainsail when a squall
blew up and carried the works off in strips.
The Captain stood to the wheel shouting orders,
we let go the halyards to lower the foresail
and take in reefs but the ropes burst or
jammed around the peak block and the foresail
blew away in ribbons, along with the three jibs.
Only the spanker managed to stay up and
the Captain hove to, keeping her underway in
the storm so as to not be drifting for shore.
The sea came across the decks and took the rail,
the bulwarks and part of the upper bridge,
all hands were engaged at the pumps to keep
her afloat; there was no food or sleep to be had,
the galley and forecastle were saturated and
the fresh water spoiled, the men getting laid up
one after another with sprains and exhaustion
as we lay in that condition 74 hours and it would
try the nerve of a mule to endure so long without rest.
When the wind moderated we got her fitted up
as best we could, mustering some old sails
stored below, bending a mainsail for a foresail
and making way for Boston, swearing we'd never set foot
on a boat again if we were able to gain the harbour.

By the time the weather ceased there was only the Chief Mate,
myself and the Captain left sound to manage the ship
and we shimmied her safe up to the pier at last,
a hard looking sight by then, but not lost.

'Taking photographs.' (1891)

Carried photographical outfit aboard
for a voyage to Cape Town,
having purchased my own from
Mr. Waites' shop in London
where I worked several months
between voyages while lodging
at Lady Ashburton's House

Second week out I sketched off
the Captain, Chief Engineer and Mate
on the starboard side
and now have all I can do to
keep up taking pictures,
the passengers willing to pay me well
for my trouble

Two days off South Africa
met the four master on which I first
crossed the pond, the *Konigsburg*
bound for England –
managed a decent portrait of her,
broad side and set with full sail
so even if the oceans take her now
she is mine to keep

'Now in Africa among the Natives.' (1891)

In vain with loving kindness
the gifts of God are strown,
the heathen in his blindness
bows down to wood and stone.

Sketches in the old mission letters suggested
these people were grey, charcoaled,
unhappy shadows slumped and frowning.
I see now they are something altogether different –
skin the colour of stained wood
and teeth bright as the keys of a church organ;
hair as rich a black as peat moss, their voices
musical and muscular, echoing thunder and rain

God's will is God's will and if I once pretended to
comprehend a portion I have since given up the lie;
I've kept good company on Africa's shore,
on the white beaches of Brazil, in China and Ceylon,
it confuses me to have shared the kindness
of liquor and song with these when some
brought up under the sound of the Gospel would
see you dead before offering a drink of water

I thought the world would make me a wiser man,
but I am merely more perplexed –
I've learned to distrust much of what I was taught before
my travels showed me different;
the faces of Africa are as dark as a night without stars,
but they are not as blind as they are pictured

'A narrow escape almost but saved.' (1892)

Aboard a Scotch boat shipping a cargo of
marble and alabaster across the Gulf of Lyons.
Three days out we came on a perfect gale,
the seas running above the mast heads
and the Captain had us clew up the topsails,
haul in the jibs and bring down the mainsail to reef it tight.
I was running out on the boom to make fast the outer jib
when the ship dropped away like a gallows door
and came up hard on a swell, chucking me
fifteen feet into the air and overboard;
I was lost but for falling into the outer jib whips
rolled four feet underwater by the gale,
like a dip net after capelin.
I hung fast to a rope as the ship rolled back,
got hold of the martingale whisker
and heaved myself in over the bowsprit to see the Captain
running about the deck with a life buoy
shouting he had lost a man.

We had a fine laugh about it afterwards –
when I climbed back aboard, they said my face was as white
as the 4 ton blocks of marble we had wedged in the hold.
But I don't remember being afraid when I fell,
only the certainty of knowing I was about to be drowned
a thousand miles from home,
and then the jib whip in my hands,
the peculiar darkness of discovering
there is nothing that is certain.

I came out of the water a different man than I had been
though I would be hard-pressed to say the difference.
The scar of that rope on my palms
for weeks after the storm had passed.

'Useful information, the Holy Lands' (1893)

Desert the colour of winter sunlight,
a yellow that is almost white, shadowless,
constant shift of sand like
a tide swell beneath your feet.
Hills on the horizon as red as blood.

The Commandments carried down Mount Sinai
by Moses in sandals, his feet blistered
by the heat of God's presence,
lettered stone scorched by the sun,
his bare hands burning.

All of this was once under water –
mountains rose from the parting flood
like the Israelites
marching out of the Red Sea
to walk parched into wilderness,
sucking moisture from handfuls
of hoar frost.

I have spent my life on the ocean,
seven years now I have worked
on the high seas,
my hands blistered by the water's salt,
my tongue thick and dry as leather.
The desert was familiar to me,
I knew something of what it
demands of a person,
what it can teach.

I understood that it is mostly thirst
that makes a place holy.

Understanding the Heart 1894-1939

'When I started trading.' (1894)

In seven years sailing I laid eyes
on the rocks of Newfoundland but twice,
skirting Cape Race shoals for Halifax
and again on the way to Boston,
looking away as quick as that
on both occasions;
I could hear her singing across the water
and stopped up my ears,
I suppose I knew I'd never be able
to leave a second time

Intending a brief visit to family last fall
I married a woman in Tomwalls Harbour,
paying the old priest three dollars
to splice us; she held me like a tree
grown through a wire fence
and I could not get away in the spring
though I said that was what I wanted

Bought a sloop and started trading
wood and coal and dry goods
around the Bay of Exploits,
gave up the sea for memories
bound as I was to the island of my birth;
I wanted an excuse to stay and found one
but a man's heart is never satisfied
and there is still a song
in my head on times that
will not let me be

'Boat Building.' (1899)

Before the snow settles in
have your wood cut and
carried to the dock yard where
you can work away at her
through the winter.

Scarf the joints to frame her out,
fit the beams, sides and stanchions,
then caulk her timber tight with
old rags or moss chinked in
with maul and chisel.
Give her a name before you
fit her out with rigging,
christen her bow with a prayer.
When the spring drives off the ice
launch her into the harbour
and hope for the best
when you let her go.

Remember this if you can:
a boat on the water belongs
to the water first
regardless of her name
or who it is that names her.

'Who can understand the heart of a man.' (1907)

He sat reading a paper until eleven,
knocked out his pipe,
doused the lamp.
His wife already in bed
he undressed in the darkness,
folding his clothes across
a chair-back.
Around midnight he turned out
to get his knife,
his wife sitting up to see
what he was about.

He had two daughters,
the eldest screamed *Daddy Daddy*
look what you have done
and he ran out of the house
to the canal where he drowned himself.
I watched them haul his body
from the water and carry him
to the dead house.

He was a stranger to me –
met him coming across from Tilt Cove
aboard the *Marion* two days before.
I slept next to him in the forecastle
and he did not stir through the night.

When he bolted from the house
he carried the knife with him
and there's no saying
where he left it.
In the mouth of the harbour maybe,
the silver blade still catching light
beneath the shallow water.

'Distance from Newfoundland.
Northernmost grave in the world.' (1913)

A cairn of stones tells the story,
broken oar and a sledge runner
roughed into a cross
where the remains of George Porter lie,
the end of an expedition to Ellesmereland
1800 miles from St. John's harbour,
the vessel found wrecked
and nearly forgotten
on the Carey Islands.

I have travelled 12000 miles
to Van Diemen's Land,
crossed the line and lost sight
of everything I had looked upon,
the North Star put out like a pauper
when the Southern Cross
appeared in the sky;
the Water Bear, the Albatross,
the South Sea Seal guiding overhead,
so many strange things that seemed
strangely familiar
as if I was visiting an old city
I knew well from maps and stories.

In Constantinople I stepped into
the Dardanelles that drowned Leander
swimming for the light of Hero's torch;
I walked the streets of Salonica
where a seller of purple and fine linens
became Europe's first Christian,
a convert of shipwrecked-St Paul,
the two of them praying together
among bolts of cloth, Lydia
was the woman's name.

George Porter lies under stone
only 1800 miles from Newfoundland
and almost further than a man could travel –
an initialled watch beside the cairn
where sailors stumbled upon it,
a notebook with the dead man's name,
how close he came
to being lost forever.

'Life and its pleasures.' (1921)

The only lesson the years have to teach
is that life is a lottery and
my name has been called a few times
when I wish it had not.

My third year trading
I engaged John Pelley of Exploits
to build me a 15 ton boat,
brought her down from
Little Burnt Bay in the spring
and went into Art's Cove
to cut a load of birch wood,
leaving her at anchor.
She was fitted with everything new
and was worth four hundred dollars
when a hard breeze of wind
took her ashore,
I sold what I could save
for ten dollars and fifty cents.

Coasted lumber between Gander Bay,
Brown's Arm and Botwood in
the little schooner *Mary March*;
she lay frozen in ice all the winter,
and a heavy sea close on
the break-up wrecked her
before I could get aboard
in the spring.

Served as master on the 47 ton
schooner *Rolling Wave*
when she parted her chains
in Deep Cove and the rocks beat
out the bottom,
keel and planks floating
out of the harbour like
life's pleasures lost,
we were lucky to get off her
before she wrecked.

The 18 ton sloop *Blanch*
came free from her anchor
on the last trip of the year,
the *Arthur Janes* struck
a rock in Dildo Run;
the *Prima Donna* we salvaged
and worked on all the winter
only to lose her on the shore again.

If Fortune shows favour
she's fickle besides;
in thirty years trading
I have owned more boats
than I could name,
and have lost almost
as many as I have owned.

'At home on a cold winter's night.
The changing scenes of Life.' (1928)

November bluster,
the night sky obscured by cloud.

On the tall ships I was taught
to steer by the stars,
took them for granted,
like a portrait of grandparents
hung in the hallway before
you came into the world.

There is a telescope on Mount Wilson
in California whose lens
weighs 4 and one half tons
and measures 100 inches across –
they say it has mapped the heavens
for hundreds of millions of miles,
that the darkness is deeper than
we ever imagined.
New galaxies and constellations
discovered every day
and it is still only
the simplest things we understand.

The speed of light exceeds
eleven million miles a minute,
it travels through space
for thousands of years after
its star has collapsed;
it is possible
that all my life I have
taken my mark by
a body that does not exist.

A chunk of wood shifts in
the fireplace,
falls;
through the window I watch
winter clouds drift and gather.

Clotted field of stars beyond them,
light rooted hard in darkness.

'An old sailor's portion.' (1932)

I am an old man now
hard aground in Twillingate
and telling tales to skeptics,
my finger dipped in tea
to sketch a map across the table.

The young ones drop by with
whiskey to hear me talk,
I give them streets
cobbled with marble in Italy,
the long spiralling line of China's wall,
the songs I learned while drinking
with the darkies in Virginia,
those sounds as old as a continent...
I can tell they don't believe
the half of it.

It's an old sailor's portion
to be disbelieved so often
that he begins to doubt himself;
the best part of my life has passed
as a shadow, and shadows are what
I am left with –
perhaps every place I have ever been
is imaginary, like the Equator
or the points on a compass.

Don't ask me what is real
when you hear me talk,
I can only tell you
what I remember.

Look down at the table.
The map has already disappeared.

'Pulling along toward the last end of
the Warp of life and the man changes.' (1935)

I can't explain why I was
never happy to stay ashore back then…
159 thousand nautical miles
I have travelled,
laid my eyes on the colours
of 32 countries around the globe
and gladly said good-bye
to them all

I used to say I loved the water,
knowing from the start
it wasn't that simple

I've sailed in seas running higher
than a ship's topyard,
watched it take down
mast and sail together
before settling into a meditative calm,
the waves like saints of God
resigned to death

When I was a boy in Twillingate
the sailors would say
the ocean is a cruel master,
but I know now it is merely
indifferent, distant,
like the stars;
that it will go on being
what it is long after other things
are lost forever in the dark –

grey horse, garlanded with foam,
at night alight with phosphor;
or lying placid on the tide swell
spangled with a map
of constellations

A Map of the Islands

This is what it means to use a map. It may look like wayfinding or a legal action over property or an analysis of the causes of cancer, but always it is this incorporation into the here and now of actions carried out in the past.

– Denis Wood, *The Power of Maps*

... a map is but one of an indefinitely large number of maps that might be produced for the same situation or from the same data.

– Mark Monmonier, *How to Lie with Maps*

What's Lost

The Labrador coastline is a spill of islands,
salt-shaker tumble of stone,
a cartographer's nightmare –
on the coastal boat 50 years ago
the third mate marked his location after dark
by the outline of a headland against the stars,
the sweetly acrid smell of bakeapples blowing off
a stretch of bog to port or starboard,
navigating without map or compass
where hidden shoals shadow the islands
like the noise of hammers echoed across a valley.

The largest are home to harbours and coves,
a fringe of clapboard houses
threaded by dirt road,
grey-fenced cemeteries sinking
unevenly into mossy grass.
Even those too small to be found on the map
once carried a name in someone's mind,
a splinter of local history –
a boat wracked up in a gale of wind,
the roof-wrecked remains of a stage house
hunkered in the lee.

Most of what I want him to remember
lies among those islands, among the maze
of granite rippling north a thousand miles,
and what he remembers is all I have a claim to.
My father nods toward the coastline,
to the bald stone shoals almost as old as light –
That was 50 years ago, he says,
as a warning, wanting me to understand
that what's forgotten is lost
and most of this he cannot even recall
forgetting

Grady I

*370   The Wolves
⊙ Grady Harbour
rth Cove   Black I
C St Nicolas   **09**
Mullins Cove
        · Bird Is
    North Hd

LABRAD⊙R SEA
(ATLANTIC OCEAN)

08

Table
Bay   Entry I   Collingham   Halfway I
                   I
        390 · Devils Lookout I   Offer Red
    South Hd   I

North
Wolf I 310 South
              Wolf I

        C Green   Ferret Is
Sand Hill Cove   North Shoal
                     Bay
        Musgrave   Indian
                  Indian 390'   Deer I
· cabins   Tickle
                      Land
    550   Narrow   Rocky   Duck
                              Bay   I
                                     · cabins

Farmer
Cove
buildings

BLACK TICKLE
349 1E
(Private)
Unmonitored

        Eagle I   Red Point   Spotted Island
                                          Run
        cabins ·   310 Island   Domino ⊙   Black Tickle
              Reeds Pd   of Ponds BLACK TICKLE
                                        57 Ⓛ 25A122.8   Roundhill
        — Porcupine   I
    968   Porcupine Bay   290 Battear Harbour
              Hr
                                         Mark Is
        cabins
                                     Porcupine I
        390 ·
                   Open B   Sandy Is
                                   Bed Hd
    500   Black Bear
          Black   Corbet I
    755 · Black River   **12**
        14   French ans   Seal I
                                Island ⊙ ⊙ Seal Islands Harbour
                                         Copper I
    755   Partridge Partridge
                          Bay Pd   552
                                     bldgs   Comfort Bight
                                     Long   Cox Hd
                                      Pd
                                             Stag I
                                     Hawke
    955   Island
        Falls   Hawke   Holloway
                   796   Harbour ⊙   Bight

                        EJ   676
                                      Stony

Naming the Islands

Inhabitants and Explorers
Iles des Esquimaux. Indian Island, Indian Bay, Indian Tickle.
Frenchman's Island. Cranford Head, Turner's Bight, Gilbert Bay.
Lac Grenfell, Tom Luscombe's Pond.
Cartwright, Cabot and Granby Islands.

No Comment Necessary
Island of Ponds, Bay of Islands.
Iles du lac, la Grande Ile.
Woody Point, Rocky Bay, Stoney Arm.
Fishing Ships Harbour.
Drunken Harbour Point.

You'll Know It When You See It
Table Island, Square Island, Narrow Island.
Saddle Island, Iles Crescent.
Chimney Tickle, Quaker Hat, Spear Point.
Castle Island.
Conical Island.

Tomayto/Tomahto
You Say Napakataktalic I say Manuel Island
   " " Tessiujalik   " " Lake Island
   " " Nanuktok   " " Farmyard Islands
   " " Wingiayuk   " " Lopsided Islands
   " " Nunaksuk   " " Little Land Island

Mostly Wishful Thinking
Belle Isle. Bonne-esperance, Baie des belles amours.
Comfort Bight. New York Bay.
Paradise.

Abandon Hope All Ye Who Enter Here
Devil's Lookout, Black Tickle, False Cape, Bad Bay.
Savage Cove, Brig Harbour.

Battle Island, Cut Throat Island. Wreck Cove.
Pointe aux morts.
The Dead Islands.

Phallic and Phallocentric
Big Island and Long Island. Cox Head. Stag Island.
Halfway Island about 10 nautical miles from Entry Island.
The Shag Islands.
Snug Harbour.
The post-coital Tumbledown Dick.

All Creatures Great and Small
Porcupine Island. Crab Island, Caribou Run, Deer Island.
Iles aux chiens, Bull Dog Island.
Seal Bight, Capelin Bay, Partridge Bay Pond.
Goose Cove, Fox Cove, Hare Harbour.
Duck, Eagle, and Gannet Islands.
The Ferrets, the Wolves. Otter Bay.
Venison Island.
Snack Island in the mouth of Sandwich Bay.

Come Again?
Haypook Island. Horse Chops Island.
Bed Head. Separation Point.
The River S-t-i-c-k-s.
Nothing Bay.

All the Way Home
Hawke Island Whaling Station, late 1930's

The *Kyle* went into Hawke's Harbour every season,
shallow bay stained the colour of wine;
storm of gulls over the water,
a racket like the noise of
some enormous machine choked with rust,
grinding to a standstill.

Went ashore to have a look one year,
the whaling room about the size
of an airplane hangar but lower,
the air inside the building bloated
with the stink of opened carcass;
the one I saw was as long as a small schooner
maybe sixty or seventy feet,
five men in cleated boots scaling the back and sides,
hacking two feet through hide and blubber
with a blade curved like a scythe;
hook and cable attached to winch
it off in strips then, as if they were
pulling up old carpet from a hallway.

A man can get used to anything, I suppose.
I tried a piece of whale meat and liked it,
although it was coarse, and stringy
as a square of cloth.
One of the whalers showed me the harpoons
up close, explained how they explode inside
the body or open up to grapple bone and tissue.
He said a big one might drag the boat
half a day past Square Islands before
they could winch in and turn for the harbour,
a narrow trail of blood on the water's surface
like a string they could follow
all the way home.

Stealing Bait
Nain, 1957

The year he came to teach at the school
someone began following the trappers' lines
through the bush, stealing bait,
setting free whatever was found alive.
There was talk of spirits and such at first,
we should have known it was just the white man.
He'd come into the classroom with bandaged hands
or a nip in his face where the foxes got at him
when he knelt to pry them loose.

An elder went down to see him,
explained how the legs in the trap
are broken, the freed animals
limping off to die of starvation
in a hole somewhere, it made no difference.

He was a crazy sonofabitch anyway,
off in the woods all alone like that,
talking to the trees. It was no surprise
he killed himself that winter,
a shotgun pushed up under his chin.
He had taken off one shoe to fire the round,
his big toe shoved into the snare
of the trigger guard, the bone
broken clean by the rifle's kick.

Cousin
Saddle Island, Red Bay c.1550

The world's largest whaling station, scores of Basque sailors hunting Rights and Bowheads up and down the coast in 16ft skiffs, six men at the oars and one straddled across the bow as they crest the back of a steaming whale, oak shaft of the harpoon hefted above his shoulder like a torch meant to light their way through night and fog. The weight of a falling man pierces the water's skin, the edgeless shape moving beneath it like a dark flame.

A speared Bowhead could drag a boat for hours, trailing blood and bellowing before it died of exhaustion or its wounds, the oarsmen rowing furiously to keep steady beside it, avoiding the piston slap of the animal's tail that could hammer the open skiff to pieces when it surfaced. Thousands hauled up in the lee of Saddle Island to be rendered every season, the enormous bodies like stolen vehicles being stripped for parts: the thick, pliant hide stretched across umbrella frames in France and Spain, the finest women in Europe corsetted with stays of whale baleen; tons of fat boiled down in copper cauldrons, a single schooner carrying 700 barrels of oil home in the fall.

The useless bones dumped in Red Bay Harbour – the curved tusk of the mandibles, hollow vertebrae, the long fine bones of the flipper: carpals, meta-carpals, phalanges, cousin to the human hand.

The remains of a hundred whalers interred on Saddle Island, their heads facing West, a row of stones weighed on their chests as if to submerge them in the shallow pool of earth, to keep them from coming up for air.

The corpses of several men often exhumed from a single grave, victims of a common misfortune. A seven man crew sometimes buried side by side, their livelihood their undoing; shoulders touching underground, long fine bones of the fingers pale as candle light folded neatly in the hollow of their laps.

Capelin Scull

What you'd imagine the sound of
an orchestra tuning up might look like,
cacophony of silver and black at your feet.
Spawning capelin washed onto
grey sand beaches in the hundreds
of thousands like survivors of a shipwreck,
their furious panic exhausted into
helpless writhing while boys scoop them
into buckets with dipnets.
They migrate all the way
from the Carribean for this,
each wave rolling onto the shore
like another bus stuffed with
passengers bound for oblivion,
limbs and heads hanging recklessly
through the open windows.

Most of them rotted on the beach
or found their way onto gardens
planted with potatoes in those days,
except for the few we dried on
window screens beside the shed,
neat rows of the tiny fish
endlessly buzzed over by houseflies
like crazy eighth notes on a staff.
Roasted them over open flame
until they were black and they tasted
much as you'd imagine burnt fish would
but we ate them anyway
head and tail together.
They had come such a long way
and given themselves up so completely
and in such an awful silence
that we felt obliged to
acquire the taste.

Water Glass
Near Domino Run, August 7th

Early evening, approaching a gate of islands;
the boat sailing effortlessly through calm
like a soul about to leave the world,
low sun navigating a placid scatter
of cloud white as pearl.
Passengers congregated above deck
praising the strangely beautiful weather.

A wind as warm as furnace exhaust lifts
an imperceptible lens of moisture that warps
our vision, the landscape of humped rock
skewed to pillars of straight, striated stone.
A shoal riding high in the Run shimmers
as the boat rolls on the tide swell,
then disappears completely
like a penny at the bottom of a water glass.
My father stares down the long flue of islands
and makes a sour face, sceptical of the wind,
predicts we're in for weather and soon.
The Americans beside us oblivious to
his dark forecast, their faces haloed by sunset.

As we steam closer the nearest rock cliffs
resolve into stumps of treeless stone,
red-faced in the failing light
like faith-healers exposed as fakes.
Out of view on the far side of the Run
the squall is picking up momentum,
the water stirred into a wicked lop,
clouds carrying darkness, a plague of sleet;
stands of low spruce on the bigger islands
bent over in the gale,
genuflecting towards the day's peace
as it abandons the blind ship.

Newfoundland Sealing Disaster

Sent to the ice after white coats,
rough outfit slung on coiled rope belts,
they stooped to the slaughter: gaffed pups,
slit them free of their spotless pelts.

The storm came on unexpected.
Stripped clean of bearings, the watch struck
for the waiting ship and missed it.
Hovelled in darkness two nights then,

bent blindly to the sleet's raw work,
bodies muffled close for shelter,
stepping in circles like blinkered mules.
The wind jerking like a halter.

Minds turned by the cold, lured by small
comforts their stubborn hearts rehearsed,
men walked off ice floes to the arms
of phantom children, wives; of fires

laid in imaginary hearths.
Some surrendered movement and fell,
moulting warmth flensed from their faces
as the night and bitter wind doled out

their final, pitiful wages.

Hunters & Gatherers

between Makkovic and Postville, August 11th

This is repression.... We forget something. And forget that we have
forgotten it. As far as we are subsequently concerned, there is
nothing that we have forgotten.   – R.D. Laing

Hunters gathered that shale, layered it
into its roughly human shape
two centuries ago, ridged spine of stone
on the highest point for miles,
raised as a guide for descendant hunters
like a gene passed down through generations,
Inukshuk overlooking the ocean
and the broad swell of inland tundra
teeming with ptarmigan and grouse.

In the ship's lounge a scatter of kids from
Davis Inlet take in a Disney film on the VCR,
an infant milks Pepsi from a baby bottle;
20 dozen beer picked from the forward hold overnight,
a wrecked assembly of Innu and Inuit strewn
in lounge seats now, smelling of booze and
smoke and mindless bewilderment,
robbed even of a sense of loss.

The blind silhouette on the horizon ignored,
like constellations stranded above a city;
one shale arm extended to point
the next hunter inland to the caribou routes,
that part of a people whose waiting
lives beyond patience.

It will stand that way for
a long time to come.

Cain
Breen's Island, 1941

My father stabbed his brother with
a white-handled pocket knife
when they were boys and working on the Labrador –
he can't recall what caused the incident
but he remembers the rage catching
like an anchor in his chest
and the look on his brother's face
when the knife hooked his leg,
bug-eyed as a cod jigged into a dory

Fifty years later, Hollis is dead
and the memory of the afternoon
my father wanted it that way
has an edge he never expected –
the details are unchanged,
a dark spatter of blood on his fist,
the three inch blade in the leg coming out clean;
but it's his brother he identifies with now,
the boy with the knife so far behind him
that he can only marvel at the darkness
and how quickly it swamped him,
his face caught on the same hooked-fish
look of incomprehension when he reaches
the part about lunging for the thigh
and stabbing ...
as if someone he thought
he could trust had turned on him,
as if he had been the one with
his back to the knife when
the blade struck home.

The Women

There was one in every fishing crew of four or five, brought along to cook and keep the shack in decent shape, and do their part with making the fish when the traps were coming up full, cutting throats or keeping the puncheon tub filled with water. They helped set the salt cod out on the bawns for drying in August, called out of the kitchen if a squall of rain came on to gather it up before it was ruined.

Most were girls whose families needed the wage, some as young as thirteen, up before sunrise to light the fire for tea and last to bed at night, the hot coals doused with a kettle of water.

Usually the girl had her own room beside the skipper's downstairs, the rest of the crew shoved into bunks under the attic eaves on mattresses stuffed with wood shavings. Sometimes it was only a blanket hung from the rafters that stood between her and the men.

When the work slowed after the capelin scull, a fiddle might be coaxed from a corner on Saturday nights, lips set to a crock of moonshine, followed by a bit of dancing, heels hammering the planks down in the bunkhouse. The single boys courted hard, they'd fall in love just to make it easier getting through the season. There was a carousel of compliments, of flirting, there were comments about the light in a girl's eyes or the darkness of her hair. There was romance of a sort to be considered: coals to be fanned alive or soused with the wet of a cold shoulder. The fire of loneliness and fatigue smouldering in the belly.

Most of it came to nothing but idle talk and foolishness, though every year there were marriages seeded on the Labrador islands, along with a few unhappier things. A child sailing home pregnant in the fall and four men swearing they never laid a hand upon her.

The Cold War
Hopedale, August 15th

Radar base raised here in the 50's at the height
of the Cold War, American soldiers hunkered in
steam-heated buildings 800' above the village,
monitoring arctic air space around the clock,
waiting for the red blip of airplanes
approaching from the north,
a nuclear warhead winging for the White House.

The glaciers of the last Ice Age clawed across
this coastline ten thousand years ago, stripping topsoil,
gouging the vulnerable land into tickles, bays, and bights,
nothing but barren stone left to stand above the Atlantic.
By November the sea is frozen, the islands raftered
together by a bridge of solid ice,
the scarred rock submerged in snow;
a man could spend months watching from this hillside
and see nothing move in the expanse of white
but the wind and what his mind imagines it sees there.

The tiny base torn down now, only the square trunks
of the radar antennae visible from Hopedale below.
The flat foundations of the barracks
left to catch rain or snow,
concrete stairs where the doors once stood
leading five steps up into nowhere –

Moravians

Hopedale Church Building est. 1771

> were we led all that way for
> Birth or Death?
>
> T.S. Eliot, 'Journey of the Magi'

Naked oak frame raised in a German field,
metallic hymn of hammers ringing across the valley,
grain of the blond wood splayed by
the driven circumference of nails.
At night the wind whispered among the bones
of the church like a restless congregation;
constellations fell through the ceiling rafters.

The location of every truss and cross-beam
recorded, carved into the wood,
the genealogy of fitted lumber mapped
from spire to base before it was taken down
and carried to the harbour mouth,
struts laid flat in the belly
of a ship for the three week journey.
Hard light of the North Star
ringing overhead at night,
marking the course across the Atlantic.

A handful of Moravians already living among the Eskimo
on the bald stone shores of Labrador,
awaiting the vessel's arrival and dreaming
the church resurrected, its spire clothed in spruce planks,
dreaming the disembodied voice of the bell sounding
over barren tundra and the word of the Gospel in
a new land driven home like a nail.

Painting the Islands

At first glance the coast of islands
is treeless, a monochrome beige or grey,
the hills in the distance flayed
or worn smooth like a whetstone worked by a knife.
Narrow valleys of green emerge from shadow
as you sail into them,
stands of dwarf spruce in thin soil,
their roots tendrilled to stone;
white antlers of snow glitter in high crevices,
meadows of moss cover the sway-backed headlands
clean as a freshly mown lawn.
In the brief three months of a northern summer
fields of White Heather and Honeysuckle
find grace enough to bloom,
bushels of blueberries ripen
in the wet of August rain.

To paint the islands properly
you have to see them up close,
to know the light that inhabits their darkness –
moments of rust and bronze in
the dull granite rock,
the Neapolitan swirl of molten lava
fissured through the grain of hillsides.

Approaching Nain, the islands
are bare and burnished black,
metallic glint of the afternoon sun
caught by long blades of mica
imbedded in the surface
and for the few minutes it takes
to sail beyond them the stones
are alive with light.

Company
Saddle Island, Red Bay, August 19th

The island would rather be left alone:
arthritic crag of stone, dry tufts of scrub,
contrary old man with his back to the world,
ignoring the steady drizzle of tourists drawn
by a minor stable of heritage sites:
Dorset midden harbouring a scatter
of bone and chipped stone tools as old
as the house of God,
the graves of Basque whalers weighted
with rows of granite rock like crude buttons
on the cold coat of the earth.
Visitors stilled by the diminishing heft
of those lives, their silence keeping company
with other, longer silences.

The island, meanwhile, is busy forgetting,
the whalers stripped of faces by a thin shroud
of acidic soil, their stone firepits fallen in
and swallowed by a dark mouth of bramble.
Abandoned freighter tilted in the lee, burnished orange
with rust, her name eaten from the bow.

Last stop, a whaler's lookout stoved in
and rotted on a bare rock ledge,
the black earth remains of wood and baleen
seeded by the wind, a patch of sod now
plush as shag carpet underfoot.
The shallow impression lodged in moss
by the weight of each new arrival
erased before the island is left behind.

The Change Islands

Earle Son's and Company (1941) Limited

Branches: Fogo, Tilting, Joe Batt's Arm, Barr'd Islands,
             Herring Neck, Change Islands

Makers of: Seavita 'Fancy' Boneless Cod Fish
             terra nova CODFISH with RICE
             Pre-cooked SHREDDED CODFISH
             Happy Cat Food!

And: LINGONBERRY SAUCE
             The tiny delectable Lingonberry grows on
             a small evergreen shrub and is picked
             in its natural habitat –
             the windswept hills of Newfoundland
             and Scandinavia.
             Serve with poultry or pork.

Earle Son's and Company (1995) Limited

Branches:

Makers of:

And:

Cataract

Breen's Island lies in the mouth of Indian Tickle, two rocks hinged by a narrow strand of beach, fused vertebrae in a long spine of water running between two larger islands. He hasn't laid eyes on the place in fifty years and hoped to this afternoon, but there's a heavy sea on as they labour through Domino Run and the Skipper won't chance the passage. Rain, and grey waves breaking on the headlands, water worrying stone. He and his son stare down through the Tickle with binoculars as the ship staggers by the northern entrance, Breen's Island out of sight behind a crook of land.

As they trace the arm of the Tickle in open water, he names the pairs of islands to port: the Gannets, the Ferrets, the Wolves. The seascape like a book of rhymes from childhood he is unforgetting in fragments. He points out the stretch of bog where they picked bakeapples in August, the deep water shoals best for jigging cod at season's end. And Breen's Island just over the cliff to starboard, as good as fifty years away. When the ship clears the arm they turn to watch the Tickle recede, passing the binoculars back and forth between them. Half a dozen tiny islands in the mouth, one revealed behind the other like a series of Chinese boxes each hidden inside the last. *Do you see it*, his son asks, and he grins uncomfortably, as if he wants to say yes for his son's sake but can't. They aren't close enough to make it out for sure. He knows they never will be. The ship heaves south on the dark swell toward Red Point, Indian Tickle slowly blurring out of focus.

The steady drift of rain like a cataract clouding his eyes.

A Note on the Text

Much of this book is a collaboration between myself and Newfoundlanders past and present. Some of the people 'speaking' here are no longer around to argue with how they've been represented, so I'd better say up front that liberties have been taken.

32 Little Stories is based on tales told to me by my Uncle Clyde, Aunt Helen, Annie Crummey, my mother, Pam Frampton, Toby O'Dea, along with a few nameless others. My own over-active imagination is responsible for a number of completely fictional pieces. More than anyone else's, though, it is my father's voice and his stories that made me want to write these things down.

Discovering Darkness was inspired by *On The High Seas*, the diary of Captain John Froude (1863–1939), published in 1983 by Jesperson Press. Born in Twillingate, Newfoundland, he worked as a fisherman, sealer and miner before spending a number of years travelling around the globe as a seaman on tall ships and steamers. The titles of all the poems are taken directly from the diary. Most of the experiences related, the references to history, mythology, science and religion, along with many of the sentiments expressed, can be found in some form or other in *On the High Seas* as well. In several pieces I have acted as much as editor as writer. But the sequence is not meant to be biography. Throughout I've been free with names, dates, places and anything else I felt the poems required.

A Map of the Islands grew out of a trip on the Labrador coastal ferry, the *MV Northern Ranger*, in August of 1995. A grant from the Canada Council made it possible for me to accompany my father on the Labrador trip and to spend some time writing afterwards, for which I'm grateful. My brother and sister-in-law put us up during stop-overs in Goose Bay, and Paul found the maps that made 'Naming the Islands' possible. My brother Stephen offered a home base in St. John's during the summer of 1995, and Peter provided invaluable computer support throughout the writing of this book.

Amber McCart offered me the use of the laptop on which many of these pieces took their first steps. Jan McAlpine suggested an epilogue. Carolyn Smart was the first to read an early version of the ms and suggested I send it to Don McKay at Brick Books. Gary Draper's eyes and ears helped me find the version that ended up between the covers. Wanda Mattson made room for me in the house in which the writing was finished. Part of what this book is belongs to her.

Some of these pieces have been previously published, often in earlier versions, in *The Capilano Review, Descant, The Fiddlehead, Grain* and *TickleAce*. Thanks to the editors. A special thanks to Robert Sherrin at *TCR* for his interest and support.

Cover art is 'Splitting Table' by David Blackwood. Thanks to David and Anita for their enthusiasm and generosity. All period photographs are from the collection of Helen Crummey. Author photo by Bob 'Buchans Shirt' Meadors. Document photos by Donna Vittorio.

Michael Crummey was born in Buchans, Newfoundland ('as far from the salt water as you can get and still be in Newfoundland') and raised there and in Wabush, Labrador. In 1994 he was the first winner of the Bronwen Wallace Award for Poetry. His writing has appeared in a broad range of magazines and anthologies. His first book was *Arguments with Gravity* (Quarry Press, 1996). He lives in Kingston.